I0210984

From Here to the Ocean

poems by

Lucie Pereira

Finishing Line Press
Georgetown, Kentucky

From Here to the Ocean

Copyright © 2025 by Lucie Pereira
ISBN 979-8-89990-218-5 First Edition
All rights reserved under International and Pan-American Copyright Conventions.
No part of this book may be reproduced in any manner whatsoever without written permission from the publisher, except in the case of brief quotations embodied in critical articles and reviews.

ACKNOWLEDGMENTS

Thank you to the following publications, and the dedicated staff and volunteers who run them, for being the first homes of many of these pieces:

"First Date" and "On his deathbed, my grandfather, a lifelong Catholic, refuses last rites" in *Sidereal Magazine*
"Alberta Summer" in *Zone 3*
"WHEN HARRY STYLES SINGS ABOUT BROWN SKIN" in *groupie mag*
"DRUNK IN AN UBER POOL, I SEE A COYOTE IN GOLDEN GATE PARK" in *Honey Literary*
"If I Was Godzilla in San Francisco" in Mason Jar Press's *Jarnal*
"Lookalikes" and "LOVE POEM FOR THE GROUP CHAT" in *The Hellebore*
"Self-Portrait as a Gemini" in *Yes Poetry*

Publisher: Leah Huete de Maines
Editor: Christen Kincaid
Cover Art: Lissa Deonarain
Author Photo: Paolo Bicchieri
Cover Design: Elizabeth Maines McCleavy

Order online: www.finishinglinepress.com
also available on amazon.com

Author inquiries and mail orders:
Finishing Line Press
PO Box 1626
Georgetown, Kentucky 40324
USA

Contents

For all the teachers in my life

First Date

Am I saying your name right?
        No, it's softer, it's sharper, it's a hundred beams of light.
        Tangle of tongue and teeth.
        Hold it in your mouth like the last bite.

What do you do for work?
        Bend at the knees and forget to reply to that email and
        sip chai in the morning. I unlock doors. Crawl
        into unfamiliar caverns.

How long have you lived here?
        A woman moves to the city. Add a thousand years in
        traffic plus a twelve second walk from her door to
        the corner store plus a month-to-month lease plus
        twenty minutes on the train from here to the
        ocean. How long has she lived in the city?

Tell me about your family.
        Whenever we posed for photos, my brothers and I would
        squeeze together
        so tightly it hurt.

Where do you see yourself in 10 years?
        Unlearning gravity,
        flirting with satellites.
        Hoping for the earth to pull me closer.

Do you want to get out of here?
        Yes.

Heirlooms

When I was born, my parents gave me
two countries and three names:
one French, one Gaelic, one Portuguese.
A borrower from the beginning,
I was destined to don new disguises each day
and wear someone else's sweaters
until I forget they're not mine.

I will hermit crab my way through the world,
knocking into seashell cities and trying them on for size.

My parents gave me three names, meaning:
light   island   &   pear tree.
They gave me air, water, and earth
wrapped me up in all the elements,
rooted me to this realm.

Alberta Summer

When we laid Zella to rest, it rained so hard
the flat streets of Taber became a river.
We all lingered in the chapel, the foyer filled
with murmurs—*how peaceful your great-grandma looked*—
while the water bulleted down.
"Weddings and funerals," my grandmother said to me,
with a shake of her head that meant:
>*Next time we meet will be at the end*
>*of an aisle like this one,*
>*either you in a white dress*
>*or me in the casket.*

I remembered our family gatherings in nearby Grassy Lake,
void of both grass and lake,
named for a body of water long since drained.
How my uncles played horseshoes in the dusty campground,
offering cold Molsons to my brothers and me before we were teens.
How we called it reunion but meant introduction—
each time, I shook hands with new parts of myself.
How the shade of my skin always gave me away,
the far-flung California cousin:
>*You must be Sheri and Anil's daughter.*

One year, a storm swept through and we drove off
through the prairie, each lightning flash glittering all the way to
    the horizon.
I wished for mountains to close me in, shot through with fear
of the danger that dared to be seen before it touched you.

The first time I saw Lake Louise,
I knew something so blue had to be magic.
I couldn't believe this was part of the same land
where my ancestors had dug roots in dry grass,
nothing to see in the yawning miles but the wind.
Did they know how close they were to this sanctum?

Once, my great-grandma flipped through her photo albums,
pointed to a black-and-white shot of herself and her sister.
They posed outside the business she'd built with her husband,
the sign reading *Henderson's Hardware.*
One girl in a wheelbarrow, the other gripping the handles—
both grinning as radiant as summer.

So this was all the reason they needed:
to find a town flat and clean as paper,
to shelter in cold days & smile in sun,
to laugh with each other & live side-by-side,
to have daughters who did the same,
holding close to the land while they waited
to see if & when & how their blood would wander.

Poem in which my white ancestors meet their brown daughter

They study the sunrise of my jaw / twilight of my skin.
I examine them, too / looking for my mother.

We are more animals / than enemies
strange creatures / with familiar pheromones.

We are quiet because / we do not know
what to ask / of each other.

We are quiet because / of all that's been altered
by years, by miles / by blood.

Finally, they ask me / what I have stolen.
I can only reply / *something I cannot give back.*

atmospheric river

silver currents carry us to the next day,
and the next. in this meal, a memory,
saffron-stained and sweet. in this house,
a history that bleeds. in this air, a silence,
greener than anything you ever knew.
green enough to make your deserts dissolve.
the landscape will close you in. in this place,
your breath is not just a bad habit. in this dark,
a question is just a question. the sky is wet and the water
is air and the atmosphere is a river and
you will open your sails and welcome the flood,
knowing that sinking wouldn't be the worst thing.

A Diaspora Poem

tastes of sticky mango sunlight, a syrupy heat
I try and fail to conjure as I soak in
these watery winter rays,
crisp and translucent as
crescents of pear, a gift from
the gnarled grey tree in the backyard.

A diaspora poem
speaks of mangroves and monsoons,
but I was born into a different kind of jungle—
one with suburbs and country clubs and
way more blonde women than genetically probable.
I should be singing saffron and chasing chai,
yet here I am shivering in my California kitchen.

And what's a diaspora poem
without aunties?
without warm curries and
grandmothers' hands? the hems of saris
swishing while spices simmer?
My grandmother sends me a package filled with
shortbread cookies and masala-spiced pecans,
tells me to text her when it arrives.
My aunties are oceans away and I
keep missing their funerals.

A diaspora poem
carries the memory of the journey,
the miles crossed,
the hopes that linger on the horizon line.
All I remember is this stolen land
I claim as home,
a land that wishes I'd return
somewhere I never began.

I try to write a diaspora poem, but
all I know is that my hair
curls differently when it's humid.
That my skin tinges golden
in a certain kind of sun.

I don't know what diaspora looks like, but
I know it runs blue through my veins.
When you cut me open it'll change color,
exposed to foreign air—
salt & iron on the tongue.

On his deathbed, my grandfather, a lifelong Catholic, refuses last rites

At midnight my mother and I sit in a Denny's, drinking cheap rosé and eating breakfast food, en route to Vancouver Island to retrieve his ashes. At the crematorium my grandmother cries, then catches herself. *It's not really him.*

Later, she shakes the urn over the blackberry brambles that border their garden, the farthest area from the house that could still be called home.
I think maybe she says a prayer. In a language unfamiliar to her ancestors, to a God they received like a Trojan horse.
My mother and I pick raspberries while we watch her, eat them from our fingertips.
My father, inside the house, calls *Popular Mechanics* to cancel his father's subscription. Under the gaze of Ganesh, a shadow perched on the piano next to my graduation photos.

The unbearable intrusion of a priest in the bedroom. Grief sheltered in the shadows of the garden. This is far too intimate for God to watch.

Sunflowers

my mother paints sunflowers inside my eyelids,
tells me to close my eyes.
tells me if I go to sleep angry,
I'll wake with a frown frozen permanent on my face.

the cat is sleeping on her belly these days and
it's cause for concern.
my mother makes with her hands,
molds ingredients into something scented evergreen.
she takes our grieving neighbor on walks,
helps him dispose of his dead wife's insulin needles.
she shows me a eucalyptus tree,
untraceable branches and mottled bark.
we perch in its boughs and become two limbs
of the same confused creature.

skin touched by lilac and lavender,
her body is more home to me
than my own strange ribcage.
watching her, I learn how to furl into myself,
how to expand into all the corners of the noise.
I am still grasping at her most elusive lessons:
how to fold a fitted sheet,
how to kiss a skinned elbow,
how to give.

WHEN HARRY STYLES SINGS ABOUT BROWN SKIN

i hum with the fever of early June,
summer baby in full bloom.

days that move like molasses,
brown hair streaked copper before autumn

and brown fingers encircled with reverse shadows,
pale where once adorned with silver.

brown skin and lemon over ice
cinnamon girl burns with spice,

melts with the sweetness of brown sugar.
and when i hear this exaltation, hear that my

brown skin is *adored*, i feel the tangerine shimmer
of every fire i walked through to land here,

a world cracked open, a world where i sway
golden in the kitchen with my love,

making magic out of coconut oil and citrus,
the tile floor glistening with spilled sunshine.

Leftovers

You hate that I forget my unfinished tea.
You find abandoned cups on every surface—
amber and cold, half-empty,
sometimes half-full.

I know that you hate this.
I know how easy it could be
to finish what I've started.
Dispose of the dredges from a morning in motion,
let the remnants circle the drain, a little cyclone of closure.
But I lead a life stitched with loose ends,
and you won't let me kiss you with lipstick on,
so I find other ways to leave echoes,
to graffiti myself onto your memory:
I was here, I was here, I was here.

So many other leftovers you love—
stained secondhand sweaters and
kitchen utensils belonging to no one,
a house stocked with souvenirs of roommates past.
I think if I'd come to you shiny and new,
you'd have hardly known what to do with me.

My undrunk tea, your magpie eyes—
how lucky to live with complaints such as these.

Goodbye to All That

A quarter-century stares me down through the narrow months and I wonder if I have the fire for it. Joan says by 28 she was too old for New York City. Last year, Tim used to laugh and say we were too young to be tired, so we danced in the late hours amid the camp of it all and we drenched ourselves in glitter. Which is really just a million microplastics that will shimmer long after we're gone. In the park I think about all the insects that are living their first and last days. They don't seem to be frantic about it. Damselflies skitter across the water, perch languidly in the sun—not far from birth, not far from death. Regret is a luxury for those with too much time on our hands. Luckily this coast has an extra moment for my mistakes. I kiss your shoulder once, twice, a third time just because I can, and to remind myself I'm not in any rush.

DRUNK IN AN UBER POOL, I SEE A COYOTE IN GOLDEN GATE PARK

Low skulking shape in the heavy night,
it moves with too much swagger to be
someone's escaped pet.
I am caged in the backseat,
stranger at the wheel and stranger to my right.
My love hangs his head out the passenger side window,
a puppy intoxicated with fresh air.

Forehead against cool glass,
I watch its loping stride,
slow motion under streetlamp strobe.
I imagine it reaching the edge of the park and continuing,
streaking its way down Market Street,
stopping to catch its breath in Union Square,
traipsing through the narrow alleys of Chinatown,
gazing up at the spire of the Transamerica Pyramid.
Who knew this human habitat could house a canine
constituency?

Red light pause and it glances toward me.
Blood spinning with gin,
my chest reverberates a lupine howl.
Together we predators worship the moon,
drenched in pheromone,
while I ache for the wild things uncontained,
wonder at the strange expanses we have chosen to roam.

If I Was Godzilla in San Francisco

I would stroll down Market Street without stepping on the cracks
and I'd squash Salesforce Tower under my heel—

> that stupid fucking dildo of a building,
> that alarmingly irregular spike on the city's
> electrocardiogram

—just grind it into the pavement and let the dust linger.

I'd scoop all the traffic from the Bay Bridge with
my pinky, like a q-tip in the groove of an ear.

Then I'd pet all the cable cars until they purred,
and I'd tilt Coit Tower just for fun,
so the tourists could take posed photos like they do in Pisa.
I would bend all the bars at Alcatraz and let the ghosts roam free.

After that I'd take a bath in Stow Lake and I'd let the ducks
nest on my kneecaps, because that would be cute as shit.

When I got hungry, I would snack on a bison or two,
and brush with a eucalyptus to freshen the breath.

At sunset I would let the frigid tide at Ocean Beach
wash over my scaly toes, and in the face of the endless waves,
I would finally know what it's like to feel small.
I would laugh when I made the snowy plovers scatter,

and I would cry because

I made the snowy plovers scatter.

Lookalikes

I'm baking blue cupcakes as the world exhales,
washing them down with mimosas like a basic bitch.
My boyfriend tells me my mole reminds him of
Marilyn Monroe,
and I wonder if I should bleach my hair,
but I think to be blonde would remind me that
beauty is pain,
or maybe pain is beauty?
Or maybe it depends—
whose beauty and whose pain.

No matter what, there are still Sundays.
I let my indoor cat explore the backyard
and he's thoroughly unimpressed,
paws at the gravel like
I was born to walk on hardwood floors, you bastards.
My boyfriend says when I smile I look like
Whitney Houston.
I wonder if I should start singing in the shower,
can't remember the last time my voice made an echo.

It's so cold and I layer myself between sheets,
while the car lights blur on the slick road.
In this light, my boyfriend tells me, I kind of look like
Kendall Jenner.
I wish that I were a few inches taller.
I think that I should probably delete Instagram.

Ice plants carpet the cliffs,
sand and ocean spread below us,
and I am breathing heavy.
My boyfriend says that I look like AOC and for once,
I reply, "I get that a lot."
I go online and buy a pantsuit patterned with stars.

LOVE POEM FOR THE GROUP CHAT

when Celia video called us
after she got her wisdom teeth out
babbling through bloody gauze,
and we laughed like it really was medicine,
laughed like we cradled a cure,
and I've never been so grateful for the Internet.

heaven is empty and all the angels are queer

I don't remember what I did
to piss off my brother
but I remember his voice
like vinegar when he declared
that I would go to hell for being a lesbian.

He was fourteen, on the brink
of his first (and only) year of Catholic school.
I was sixteen, a few months shy
of my first kiss with a girl
who taught me about the Kinsey scale,
assured me she felt like a one,
maybe two at most,
bicurious at best.
I've never been good with numbers—
four is my favorite,
but sixes seem to follow me everywhere,
an omen inscribed in my birthdate.

I've never been one for absolutes,
but if hell tastes like fruit-flavored liquor
on someone else's tongue,
then I have no use for heaven.
It must be a lonely place,
because all the angels are here,
dancing through the night at El Rio,
eyes lined with perfect wings.
They know that flight can't always set you free.
The saints are parading down Castro Street,
and all the miracles we need are yet to come.

I can count my sins like cents,
but I won't pay any penance
for the times I've held a body sacred.
If paradise won't have me when I die,
I'll find it here, where we smile
under the flames on city sidewalks,
where we forgive and forgive,
and forgive and keep going
like siblings do, hurt after hurt—
no confessions required.

Self-Portrait as a Gemini

It's something you can't make heads or tails of. I scorn nicknames but adorn myself in the misspellings. On my fake ID I was Lucy with a y and that bitch was a mess but at least she managed to tuck me into bed each night. Okay, so that's not true—more often than not she'd curl up on the floor after crying into the toilet bowl, but always without fail she'd shimmer her way home. Plastic Arizona license in the back pocket of her skinny jeans. That's beside the point. The point is now I spell my name backwards so I can read it in the mirror. Now I sketch myself in antonyms and pile on contradictions to keep warm. That's the shine of it. That texture you can't pin down. It's the clinking glasses at the dinner party and the talking shit in the backseat on the way home. It's the traffic light glimmer on the car windows. The mystery in the multitudes. The darkened sand exposed in the ebb that still remembers the liquid freedom of the flow.

the good news

rain pelts the freeway as neon spells out what's to come.
we are speeding across county lines, cobbling together
an instruction manual for the unknown.
scuttling for shelter like sand crabs, our rocks overturned.

we keep counting until we forget what we've lost track of.
after one hundred, numbers become
liquid unfathomable, impossible to grasp.
we become witness to a time as red as stars.
the good news is this will all be over someday.

today the sky wears a closed-mouth smile
and i wait for her to show her teeth.
today the almond blossoms cloud the central valley
like a perfect storm.

sometimes we can't look away,
even knowing that the seeing will undo us.
even when our eyes pinprick into glaciers.
we place our fragile faith in each other,
as naive as it is necessary.
don't hurt me, please,
even though you can.

i reach for a pen while the epilogue unwrites itself,
vanishes into infinite numbers that slip away,
coin-silver fish glinting in the deep.

the good news is,
this will all be over

someday.

Poem for the walk home

I am trying so hard
to be alive to everything.

The days gape open, wide-mouthed.
I tuck a few small truths in my pockets like pennies,
as quicksilver seconds slip over each other in rivulets.

Early evening—the deer eat apple branches
from my outstretched hands.
Day breaks and recognizes me.
Late morning—my chest is full of broken windows.

In the surface of each passing airplane,
I look for my own face.
I am searching for something diamond to break my teeth on.

Tonight I will grin right back at the Cheshire cat moon,
reach toward tenderness,
and wish that my palms could soak up this suffering.

Sometimes it feels neon and
sometimes it doesn't.
Even now, the universe never tells me no.
Even still, I keep asking.

With Thanks

Many thanks to the organizations and people who have made this work possible:

The team at Finishing Line Press for making this chapbook a reality.

Jason Bayani, Giovanna Lomanto, and Rita Mookerjee for their kind words.

The San Francisco literary spaces that have shaped me: 826 Valencia, Kearny Street Workshop, Happy Endings, Quiet Lightning, Litquake, and more.

My incredible community of friends and family who have supported me as a writer and a person.

Paolo, my harbor & hearth.

Lucie Pereira (she/her) is a writer and educator from the San Francisco Bay Area. Her work has appeared in *Honey Literary, the Hellebore, Zone 3,* and *Yes Poetry,* among others. She has received fellowships from Kearny Street Workshop's Interdisciplinary Writers Lab and Rooted & Written. A graduate of Emerson College with a BA in Writing, Literature, and Publishing, she recently completed an MA in Creative Writing at University College Cork. She is a co-founder of the reading and food pop-up series Kitchen Table, a poetry reader for *Split Lip Magazine,* and an educator who has taught writing at various organizations including 826 Valencia, Children's After School Arts, and the Elder Writing Project. *From Here to the Ocean* is her debut chapbook.

www.ingramcontent.com/pod-product-compliance
Lightning Source LLC
Chambersburg PA
CBHW022101080426
42734CB00009B/1451